STUDY GUIDE FOR PREPARING FOR THE INTERNATIONAL
HARVEST

STUDY GUIDE FOR PREPARING FOR THE INTERNATIONAL
HARVEST

Dr. Trent Lambert and Dr. J. Randolph Turpin
Contributors

DECLARATION PRESS

Study Guide for
Preparing for the International Harvest

Copyright © 2021 by Kenneth L. and Pauline E. Grunden
All Rights Reserved

Contributors
Dr. Trent Lambert and Dr. J. Randolph Turpin

This material may not be reproduced in any form without the expressed written permission of the author and Declaration Press.

Scriptures marked NIV are taken from the Holy Bible, New International Version®, NIV®. Copyright © 1973, 1978, 1984, 2011 by Biblica, Inc.™ Used by permission of Zondervan. All rights reserved worldwide. The "NIV" and "New International Version" are trademarks registered in the United States Patent and Trademark Office by Biblica, Inc.™

Scripture taken from the Modern English Version. Copyright © 2014 by Military Bible Association. Used by permission. All rights reserved.

Cover Design by Jonathan Zajas

ISBN-13: 978-0-9983102-8-2

Contents

	Preface: How to Use the Study Guide	i
1	Introduction	1
2	The Emerging of an Upcoming Missionary	5
3	The International Church	11
4	The Challenge of Living in Foreign Environments	17
5	International Ministry Opportunities	21
6	Cultural Adaptation	32
7	Serving Internationally: a Major Commitment	41
8	Fulfilling the Great Commission—God's Command	48
9	Getting Started in Ministry	55
10	The Purpose of a Prayerful Life	60
11	Conclusion	65
	Addendum: Chapter Scriptures	69

Preface

How to use the Study Guide

The purpose of this study guide is to coincide as an additional study resource to the textbook, *Preparing for the International Harvest*. The objective is to help present and future missionary workers follow the leading of the Holy Spirit to accomplish their God given destinies to reach internationals in a wide variety of ways. The textbook and study guide discuss various topics that the missionary may encounter. The study guide is applicable for personal study with the book, missionary training classes, small group studies, and academic courses (on campus or online) at various levels.

Each chapter of the study guide begins with Key Concepts and Learning Objectives. These learning objectives are major points from the textbook with a summary of explanation. At the end of chapter there are four assessments that can be utilized as talking points or assignments. The assessments at the end of each chapter include Prayer Points – key areas to pray for in relation to the content of the chapter. There is a Devotion at the end of each chapter that allows for personal insight and scriptural application. There are chapter reflections that analyze objective truths shared within each chapter correlated with a subjective component that allows for critical thinking connecting personal insights. The last assessment at the end of each chapter is a formatted paper, essay or plan that allows for application and study into personal interests within the themes of study of the chapter.

Depending upon the context of the event or gathering, assessments can be utilized as points of discussion and prayer, necessary learning activities or gradable assignments. The study guide is intended to be used in conjunction with the book. The study guide examines the material of the book in smaller sections with focus on reader interaction and application.

Chapter 1

Introduction

Key Concepts and Learning Objectives

1. The Challenge – Go Prepared

As global economies expand, a greater number of people are going abroad to work, to minister, and to teach, but they are not adequately prepared for overseas assignments in their non-native culture. Commitments to work and to minister in a foreign country should lead God's people to seek practical training and formal education in basic textual courses for improvement in understanding the Bible and its spiritual truths. Those called to live abroad should be more fully prepared for opportunities in ministry. They should complete practical classroom training for Christian service, including instruction in how to teach unbelievers, an understanding of evangelism methods, skill in developing Bible study materials, knowledge and awareness of family health and nutrition, how to lead Bible studies and how to gain knowledge about the new culture.

Further preparation for foreign service is necessary in the following areas:

- Native language and interaction in the host country
- Knowledge and insights about customs and culture differences
- Cross-cultural training and spiritual preparation
- Readiness skills and correct attitudes to live and minister abroad
- Team building skills with other internationals

- Preparation for developing international ministry and missions
- Communication etiquette of another culture
- Coping strategies, adaptation, and survival in a foreign culture and country
- Acceptance by a host culture, after entering a new culture
- Skills and appreciation for another culture
- A knowledge of world missions and church preparation
- The Biblical basis of missions and world evangelism
- Managing conflict and problem resolution
- Career related skills and talents for teaching and ministering to national people

As a result of inadequate preparation, training and education, many Internationals experience undue stress, disappointment and dissatisfaction with salaries, a level of support raised, living conditions, the culture and the length of time for inconveniences related to shopping, banking and other routine tasks, to name just a few components. Missionaries become weary because of the stress brought about by day-to-day encounters with the unfamiliar culture and language barriers in addition to the tasks at hand.

2. Focusing on God's Mission

God's people who are called to minister and serve abroad must become more adequately prepared, humbling themselves, shedding arrogant, western pride, and becoming servant leaders and team builders with people of their own culture. When this is achieved, the results are:

- A more productive and longer stay in a foreign country
- More effective ministry for building and expanding the Kingdom of God
- A more positive experience for their calling to Kingdom building

- Improved focus on calling and definition of God's command to serve
- Spiritual growth and enhanced personal development
- Improved teambuilding skills with nationals and Internationals
- More harmonious relationships and cooperative ministry for the advancement of the Gospel
- Improved acceptance of nationals and international people
- Improved understanding and acceptance of national people, their culture and customs
- Skills and career-related objectives developed as they serve
- Hearing from God as to His mission to accomplish His goals

3. Responsibility for Training Up God's Servants

Our thinking must be expanded to include preparation and training for short-term missions' personnel, workers called abroad and all people who are called for international ministries and missions regardless of the tasks at hand. The church should be current in all areas of missions and become more effective in identifying, counseling and preparing God's people called abroad for the Lord's work.

The Biblical mandate to all Christians is to take and spread the Gospel everywhere. *"Go therefore and make disciples of all nations, baptizing them in the name of the Father and of the Son and of the Holy Spirit."* (MEV, Matthew 28:19)

Prayer Points:

1. Pray to see where God may use you in the narrative of world/international missions.
2. Pray for churches to enhance their training for missionaries.
3. Pray for your local church and missions' organizations.
4. Pray as to how you will support missions prayerfully and financially.

Personal Devotion:

Using a passage from scripture write a 100-word devotion that depicts the importance of personal preparation for ministry.

Discussion Points:

1. From the list of areas that missionaries need preparation in, pick three that you feel are the most important and why you feel that way. Respond in 100-150 words.
2. From the section on Focusing on God's Mission what are some areas that might cause you to lose focus or become stressed and become distracted limiting kingdom productivity in your life? Respond in 100-150 words.
3. The Great Commission is the standard by which New Testament believers engage missions. What does Matthew 28:19 mean to you in your personal walk and mission with God? Explain as much as you can as the Lord is leading you currently. Respond in 100-150 words.

Reflection and Application Essay:

In a 3-page paper using MLA, APA or Turabian formatting write about the need to prepare missions workers prior to going or relocating to an international location. In addition, use an Old Testament and New Testament passage illustrating that importance. Lastly, in your opinion what would a six-week preparation class look like and what information would be taught? Conclude your paper with some key concepts from Chapter 1 dealing with being prepared, focusing on God's mission and training that can be applied to your life now. Do not simply list them but explain why these concepts are applicable to you.

Chapter 2

The Emerging of an Upcoming Missionary

Key Concepts and Learning Objectives

1. A World to be Evangelized

The practice of God's missionary flying to foreign countries to do a great evangelistic event will soon be a thing of the past. The age of nationals leading their people to salvation is unfolding *and will become the new norm.*

Schools of Ministry are being established around the world for Nationals to learn to lead and be trained and equipped, so they can then go on to impact the lives of others through the ministering of the Gospel of Jesus Christ. The Nationals will go on to teach and train millions more of their own people. There is a domino effect that takes place.

When the Nationals are trained, they establish:

- Churches
- Ministries
- Businesses
- Jobs

2. The Fields are Ready

The church sends out its missionaries to communicate the Gospel across cultures and geographical boundaries to establish self-sustaining churches among all people for the glory of God. Today, there are at least four billion people who do not consider themselves "Christian" and nearly half who have never heard of Jesus Christ.

- The un-evangelized world makes up of 26 percent of the world.
- In the 10/40 window there are 62 nations, 3.4 billion people, 97 percent of the least evangelized people groups.
- The Evangelized non-Christian world consists of 41% of the world.
- The Christian world consists of 33 percent of the world's population.
- Born-again Christians range from 6 - 11 percent of the world's population.

3. Workers Must Have Appropriate Training

Our thinking must be expanded to include preparation and training for short-term missions' personnel, workers called abroad and all people who are called for international ministries and missions regardless of the tasks at hand. The church should be current in all areas of missions and become more effective in identifying, counseling and preparing God's people called abroad for the Lord's work.

The development and training of upcoming missionaries includes the following:

- Spiritual Development – personal discipline, victorious living, godly character, spiritual warfare, family practices, and financial responsibility

- Biblical Soundness – basic Bible knowledge, theological orientation, hermeneutics, biblical inerrancy, evangelism and discipleship

- Cultural Adaptation – cultural anthropology, sociology, language and cross-cultural communication, and acceptance into foreign community

- Worldview Interaction – cross cultural communication, linguistics, worldview studies, and apologetics

- Interpersonal Tact – cross cultural interpersonal communication, experience with differing cultures, Christian diplomacy, conflict resolution, servanthood and life-long learning about international cultures

- Communications Skills – understanding a message, teaching skills, pulpit presentation, and speaking for maximum understanding

- Managerial Skills – management skills, computer skills, teamwork skills, opportunity planning, project management, and planning and goal setting

4. Categories of Missionaries Today

Missionary service is the most demanding and dynamic initiative in Christian ministry today. It begins with people being sent out, people reaching people, and people developing people for ministry. The ministry can be summarized as move in, win over, build up, hand over, and move on.

- Traditional Missionaries – Full-time personnel are supported financially by churches.

- Nonresidential Missionaries – A career foreign missionary who serves a single un-evangelized population.

- Tentmaker Missionaries – Tentmaker missionaries provide their own financial support through employment in various fields of service.

- Bi-vocational Missionaries – The skills in other professions are in demand within those nations, so they enter to work under a different professional identity.

- The Upcoming Missionaries – The missionaries that Western churches seek today are not so much pioneers as partners and participants for a common cause of spreading the Gospel.

5. Work of Existing International Missionaries

- Building churches
- Training of students in Bible colleges
- Evangelistic meetings
- Christian family conferences
- Global leadership conferences
- Family and youth conferences
- Bible colleges
- Bible institutes
- Distribution of Bibles
- Children's homes
- Computer training centers

6. God's Mission with a Vision, Called to Serve

The six-year South Korea goals that God had for us are:

- Serve as head of the leadership team in an International Christian School in Seoul, South Korea, our initial experience in serving abroad.
- Reach Korean nationals and world Internationals for Christ, while ministering and serving on the campus of an International Christian University.
- Plant an International English Worship service within a Korean church with national pastors, attendees were Korean nationals, world Internationals, USA business people and Korean and international young people, 100 in attendance.
- Teach Bible to Korean national teachers at church, visited public schools, talked to the school children.

- Implement a "men of the sea" soul winning ministry on the major ocean liner ships
- Plant a Korean after school study program

Prayer Points:

1. Pray to see how you can be involved to train nationals in their own country.
2. Pray for the non-Christian and unevangelized world to have an encounter with Jesus Christ.
3. Pray for greater opportunities and increased training for preparation for missions' outreaches.
4. Pray what category of mission's paradigm the Lord might be leading you along with at least a 5-year plan.

Personal Devotion:

Identify a passage of scripture that depicts the Lords' leading and future directive of missions work in your life. Explain this passage and its meaning to you in about 100 words.

Discussion Points:

1. Give a biblical example of nationals being trained to make impact on the lives of others. Respond in 100-150 words.
2. Identify a couple of areas from the list of development and training for upcoming missionaries that you think is overlooked and needs to be delivered better. Why did you choose them and how could they be delivered better to upcoming missionaries? Respond in 100-150 words.
3. After looking at the list of the work of international missionaries, in your opinion in our current culture which category of missionary would be most effective to accomplish those works and why? Respond in 100-150 words.

Reflection and Application Essay:

In a 3-page paper using MLA, APA or Turabian formatting identify a city, country or region in the 10/40 window and design a 5-year plan to reach that area. Identify the major areas of training needed for the missionaries, the best category of missionary to reach that location and 3-5 key works to be established in the location. Write a paragraph or two about the background of your selected location to show context to your missionary approach.

Chapter 3

The International Church

Key Concepts and Learning Objectives

1. Multicultural, Multi-denominational, Diversity

The international church as understood in this context is a church located in a foreign country. The international service is planned and arranged with regard to the diversity in the congregation. The church of Antioch was a model of the international church, which had both a local and an overseas focus on missions. The Antioch-type church simultaneously reaches various locations and groups with the Gospel in word and deed.

2. Strength Through Diversity

The better we are at understanding and interpreting culture, the more we will appreciate others, resulting in the breaking down of cultural walls. The more authentic relationships that we can cultivate, the greater will be our ability to communicate God's truths. These are key aspects of being a "World Christian."

Three commitments characterize the World Christian and should be characteristic of every Christian:

- Committed to God's purpose for His world
- Committed to God's people who are to carry out His purpose
- Committed to working out God's purpose in daily life[1]

---

[1] Robin Thomson, *World Christian* (Oxford: Lynx/St. John's Extension Studies, 1992) in Gaukroger, 13.

Appreciation of diversity and an understanding of it, an open and willing heart, submitting to God's authority, putting aside our pride and our own agendas, and developing a love for all people in God's world will bring true success and commitment to God's calling and purpose for international ministry.

3. The Differences Between Western and Asian Cultures

The differences between Western and Asian cultures:

- The West is time-oriented
- Asia is event-oriented
- Often Asian students come to class late without thinking anything about it, or they come to church late
- The Western missionary expects promptness on the job, punctuality in coming to class, and faithfulness in arriving at church on time.
- Time-oriented people make decisions quickly
- Event-oriented people take as much time as necessary to deliberate and reach consensus.
- The West is crisis-oriented
- Asia is not crisis-oriented
- The West is task oriented
- Asia is people oriented

4. Local and Overseas People in the Congregation

The international congregation is made up of various groups of people: Westerners who are short-term and long-term, which may include students, diplomats, domestic workers, educators, businesspeople, and nationals who are citizens of the country. One does not become transformed into a missionary worker just by going abroad. "Work where you are, so you can work where you're sent" is a good motto.

5. The Mission of Christ

The responsibility of the international congregation is:

- to focus on God and His Word.
- to engage in relationship building with nationals (and other Internationals).
- demonstrate love for all of God's people.
- provide a friendly place for people to worship and have fellowship.
- provide encouragement to God's servants to be fully effective in its mission of serving Internationals.

6. Social and Personal Adjustments

The fundamental sociological need of most foreigners is the need to establish an identity and to be accepted in the community. The international pastor can assist in integrating international people into the host culture and providing stability within a home-like, caring environment.

The Apostle Paul's writings on differences that endanger unity:

- Romans 5:5-6
- Romans 12:10
- Romans 14:1
- Romans 14:13
- Romans 14:19-20
- Romans 15:7
- Philippians 2:3-4

7. Making Time for Prayer and Bible Studies

Mid-week services have been replaced with home fellowship groups. Because the community is spiritually diverse, a focus on the exposition of Scripture rather than denominational traditions is vital in Bible studies and sermons.

Midweek services provide:

- Study of the Bible
- Fellowship

- Prayer
- Encouragement
- Overall spiritual growth
- Refreshing
- Evangelism

8. Congregational Turnover

International congregations often experience a high rate of turnover. This is where church growth principles must be carefully applied. Maintaining a low "turnover" church is possible if the focus is on people and if the basics of the Christian life are stressed... Dealing with turnover is one of the most significant issues in the international church.

Methods to Deal with Turnover:
- build an excellent church foundation for the international people
- establish church programs
- train indigenous leaders
- provide historical information to newcomers

9. Task-oriented versus People-oriented

The differences between task-oriented and people-oriented missionary personnel are an important consideration for the international church. For mission work, the most productive missionaries (i.e., task-oriented missionaries) may not be the best people to send to interaction-oriented non-Western cultures. The missionary is sent to people to serve them, to minister to them, and to communicate God's love for them. Building relationships and devoting time for personal interaction is essential to ministry. Task-oriented individuals must allow time for interactions with people and not drain time and energy to continual tasks.

10. Planning the International Service

The international service should be kept simple with structure and a sense of formality. Consistency in format from service to service is important.

Essentials for international service planning:

- Develop team approaches to planning
- Services should be planned with a view toward involving people and encouraging participation
- Pastoral sermons should address the needs of people
- Create a ministry for internationals to minister and to worship in their native English language

11. Attendance Patterns

Most international church attendance is erratic. During the summer months, the attendance of Internationals could drop off to less than half, which can be very frustrating. Internationals visit other countries, travel within the host country, return home to visit family, or study at home or abroad.

This period of "down time" can be a time for:

- renewing
- training
- developing closer relationships with those who are present
- to focus on new ministries

Prayer Points:

1. Pray for a culture of unity in the presence of diversity.
2. Pray against spiritual powers and distractions that would detour your spiritual commitment to the mission.
3. Pray for favor that missionaries have opportunities to have identity and community in foreign cultures.
4. Pray for protection and effectiveness over international congregations and services.

A Study Guide for Preparing for the International Harvest

Personal Devotion:

Identify a passage of scripture that describes a task-oriented person and a people-oriented person. Give a scripture/narrative for each. How are you oriented? Give a personal example.

Discussion Points:

1. Give the historical and biblical background of the Church at Antioch and how is was a multi-cultural church. Respond in 100-150 words.
2. Describe a couple of ways that you practice strength through diversity in your personal life and ministry? Respond in 100-150 words.
3. After reading the section on Attendance patterns identify a couple other ideas that could help attendance or minister to those that are left? Could current uses of technology help with this? Respond in 100-150 words.

Reflection and Application Essay:

Focus on the section Social and Personal Adjustments. In a 3-page paper using MLA, APA or Turabian formatting use the passages mentioned in Romans as the foundation, create a current paradigm using current tools to integrate international people into the host culture and provide stability within a home-like, caring environment. Be creative and think out of the box. Try to identify 2-3 methods and discuss how they would work to accomplish the integration goal TODAY.

Chapter 4

The Challenge of Living in Foreign Environments

Key Concepts and Learning Objectives

1. Blending into and Adapting to a New Culture

Many international people have problems adjusting to a new culture. Perhaps they do not want to give up their own customs and culture temporarily, nor do they wish to blend into a host culture. Internationals usually will work in the local culture, but retreat to their own culture, as they live in their homes or in an international community. Perhaps they are not interested in the new culture or do not know how to adjust and blend into the new culture.

The lack of blending with national people and fitting into a foreign culture goes back to:

- Inadequate preparation
- A lack of knowledge in language and culture
- Many of them did not have a desire to learn the language and fit into the culture.
- It may merely be a person's recognition that he or she is not yet ready or prepared for a cross-cultural ministry experience.

A typical reaction to extreme cultural anxiety is withdrawal. By withdrawing and not participating in the lives and culture of the nationals, friendships and relationships, as well as ministry opportunities are hindered.

2. Accepting Cultural Change

Internationals who experience withdrawal on the mission field may reject the host culture and glamorize their own culture. Rather than going home, the foreign person must make a conscious decision to adapt. It is the little things that cause frustration.

Internationals should never imply that their own cultures are superior and that others are inferior. All cultures have strengths and weaknesses. Nationals may become critical of Westerners' because of:

- Intense individualism
- Pride
- Lack of respect for elders
- Their view as a superior culture

3. Adapting to the Foreign Culture

Internationals must adapt to a foreign culture quickly by integrating into the culture and appreciating the fine points of local people. They should develop a mindset and proper skills to function while transferring Biblical and spiritual truths to people in the host culture.

People who are called abroad will be successful if they learn to:

- Focus on the mission and purpose for going abroad.
- Expect challenges, obstacles, barriers, discomforts and spiritual warfare.
- Adjust their thinking on living conditions, comforts of home, normal ways of doing things, methods of transportation, shopping patterns and habits, and time it takes to get around.
- Not expect much positive reinforcement, verbal or written recognition.
- Expect miscommunications but try to reduce them.

- Not expect nationals to understand their thinking or ways of doing things.
- Pray, commit purpose to God daily, focus on God, and rely on Him and the Holy Spirit for evangelism and communications.

The foreign settler adapts to the host culture with the intention of becoming a permanent resident of the host culture by:

- Many who marry into a culture fit into this category
- Some who come as tourists have extensive contact with the host culture for a brief period of time. These tourists may be short-term job holders, individuals on vacation, or on a study program that requires much contact with the host culture.
- Others are long-term missionaries. Relationships with other foreigners can either be primary or secondary.

Prayer Points:

1. Pray for a cultural cohesiveness for internationals to engage the culture they are ministering in.
2. Pray against any demonic strongholds that would inhibit culture cohesiveness for internationals.
3. Pray for physical, emotional and spiritual strength of internationals to stay true to the mission and plan of God.
4. Pray for favor and open doors of opportunity for international to establish relationships and position to share the message of Jesus Christ.

Personal Devotion:

Write a brief encouragement to a frustrated international using a couple scriptures to uplift their faith and to gain proper perspective of the faithfulness of God. This devotion should be 100-150 words.

Discussion Points:

1. What could be done in missionary preparation to better train internationals on blending and adapting to new cultures? Respond in 100-150 words.

2. Acts 17 depicts a ministry opportunity for Paul at Mars Hill. Describe how Paul adapted to the culture to be effective in presenting the Gospel. Respond in 100-150 words.

3. What are a couple other ways not mentioned, that an international could do to adapt to a foreign culture? Explain your responses. Respond in 100-150 words.

Reflection and Application Essay:

Identify a country of interest that you have to do missions work. In a 3-page paper using MLA, APA or Turabian formatting discuss some of the presuppositions that this country has about Western culture that could be a hurdle to cross. Identify some of the physical and spiritual hurdles that would be incurred and how to possibly overcome them. Lastly, using the culture of the foreign nation put together a personal plan to overcome cultural anxiety and withdraw.

Chapter 5

International Ministry Opportunities

Key Concepts and Learning Objectives

1. Preaching, Teaching and Evangelizing in the English Language

Many ministries exist or can be developed by Internationals who have made a commitment to overseas ministry and missions. One of the most rewarding and fulfilling ministries is working in the International church preaching and teaching God's Word, training young National pastors in key significant areas to strengthen international ministries and their own ministry within their congregation. Some of the areas include:

- Praise and worship
- Praying and reading scripture in English
- Bible studies
- Team building
- Planning and goal setting,
- Special programs and services
- International cultural exchange

One of the greatest blessings in overseas ministry is establishing an international English-speaking church and international ministries within the local Korean church. Missions is not complete without forming congregations. We need to disciple new believers by bringing them to the church which is going to be responsible for ongoing evangelism.

2. Planting a Church within a Church

Conducting international worship services within an existing Korean church has many benefits as opposed to an independent startup church. Some of the benefits include:

- No building costs and overhead expenses
- No burden of raising money for church operations
- No support to raise for paying salaries of pastors
- Pre-existing presence as a well-known, funded and established church in the community

International ministries provide Christian teaching ministry opportunities for:

- Christian students (international and native)
- A ministry to the men of the sea on the ships coming into harbor
- Sunday School for children
- Expansion into other Asian countries with the Gospel
- English language and computer instruction
- Local evangelism
- Bible studies
- International outreach
- Building teamwork with local national pastors

It is useless to win people to Christ and then leave them on their own without discipleship. We need to disciple new believers by bringing them to the church which is going to be responsible for ongoing evangelism.

3. Led by the Holy Spirit

Our communication must be clear and relevant to the customs of the people, so they can understand. Sometimes, we bring rejection and persecution upon ourselves by not praying enough for clear, Holy Spirit led speaking, teaching, and outreach. Our goal must be to build up the unity and fellowship of the body of Christ. To achieve that goal, we must always consider others better than ourselves. Our position is to be that of a servant.

4. International English Worship Service in the Korean Church

The primary purpose in having an English worship service is so the Internationals will have a place to worship in a language they can understand while ministering and residing in a foreign country. However, the service can also be attractive to many Korean nationals who want to learn more about Christianity and have experiences in the English language from an international person.

The following are key points from our experiences for developing an effective English worship service for international people in a foreign country worshiping with Korean nationals in their second language:

- Foreign and national greeters for the service
- Easy to read church bulletins in the English language
- Key points of the sermon written in English
- Leaving blanks on the paper for writing or filling in key words and concepts
- Speaking more slowly with clear pronunciation
- Using simpler words
- Repeating key concepts of the message
- Using power point or technology for examples and key points of the sermon, Scripture, and words to the songs.

In administering the English worship service, it is important to remember to do the following:

- Develop a team of leaders for accountability, spiritual protection, authority, prayer and support from the national pastors and elders;

- Establish a working relationship with international people; communicate, review the ministry, pray and worship together.

- Develop an intercessory prayer team to pray for the service on a specific day, include Internationals and Korean national's prayer in English or in the native language of the country.

- Develop a praise and worship team, conduct weekly practice sessions at the church, and practice in the English language.

- Spend time with people who will share testimonies and blessings in the service, pray, read Scripture, or make announcements.

- Spend ample personal time preparing the sermon and praying for the service.

- Assemble a team of spiritual leaders for regular prayer meetings even during the services, social time for brainstorming and review, team building, and integration of the national church leaders into the English worship services

5. English Bible Studies and Prayer in the Church, on Campus, or in Homes

Bible studies are very necessary for spiritual growth and can be presented either at the church or at someone's home. The weekly studies help to meet the needs of Internationals by:

- Offering continued study of the Bible
- Fellowship and friendship
- Support group while living in a foreign country
- Helps the newcomers in the foreign field with cultural adjustment and adaptation

Integrated Bible study groups could be started in the local church with local people for fellowship and spiritual growth. Church support is necessary, as the local church also benefits from the Bible studies with increased attendance at the services. Example Bible studies are:

- Meeting with professors at the local Christian university
- Meetings on the military bases
- Kids English Bible Study (KEBS)

6. Teaching English as a Ministry in the Local Church

Another ministry opportunity is teaching English classes in the local church as an outreach of the International church. Teaching will provide an opportunity to share the Gospel with the nationals in an atmosphere of friendliness and curiosity about the international language and culture.

When teaching English in the church, always integrate it with spiritual truth and develop the spiritual context as well as academic learning. Teaching English, in addition to the Bible studies, is an excellent way to present the Gospel of Christ and teach who Jesus is. Additional classes in the church can be formed for evangelism purposes with nationals who are outside the local church. In addition to teaching English, there are opportunities to teach:

- Biblically related courses
- Business courses
- General education courses or specialty courses

7. Teaching English as a Ministry in the Christian University

Teaching at a Christian university opens many opportunities to share the Gospel in and out of class. At these Bible studies, students are encouraged to attend the campus church or to attend the English worship service at the International church.

8. Leadership and Teaching as Christian Service

Other opportunities for Christian service and witnessing exist at the Christian university. Some examples are to serve in are:

- Office of International Relations
- Department of Language and Education

A Study Guide for Preparing for the International Harvest

9. Korean National Students Outreach Throughout Asia as a Ministry

For the purpose of a missionary outreach, Korean Christian university students will often travel to other countries in Asia to teach English and computer technology to Asian nationals and to introduce the Gospel and share Christ to students and their parents.

In newly independent countries, tentmakers provide valuable services. Tentmakers who are educators, business and trained professionals offer their skills and services to assist in the economic development and growth of the country. These services are not offered in exchange for souls, but in a genuine spirit of servanthood. English as a Second Language (ESL) has become a popular avenue of service for many tentmakers in Asia. Bible studies are a more relaxed way of learning English and students acquire real skills

10. Sharing Christ as You Go

A common question asked is, "Why are you here?" My typical answer is that I came to share the Gospel, education and experience with the people and that God told me to go abroad and serve people spiritually. Many opportunities for in-depth discussions about God take place inside and outside of the classroom.

11. Local Outreach, Co-laboring with Korean Pastors and Missionaries

When God's word is preached, people respond and accept Christ no matter where it is. Many souls were won to Christ at the church and on the ships. The men of the sea come from many different countries, and most of them spoke English, so they attended the English worship services at the International church on Sundays. On Saturdays, the Christian university's international and Korean students joined with a Korean missionary and us to visit the men of the sea who were on the large ocean vessels.

12. Evangelism on the Military Bases – Developing Relationships

At the military bases, there are opportunities to have Bible studies and to witness to the soldiers while they are downtown or in a restaurant. Street evangelism plays a significant part in getting people to attend the international church, to participate in Bible studies, and to build friendships.

13. Ministry to Public School Teachers

Teaching English and methodology to elementary teachers from local Korean elementary schools is also an opportunity to share customs and culture, as well as to develop many friendships The teachers are invited to attend the English worship services, and many of them come there out of curiosity or to take advantage of hearing spoken English.

14. Bible Study Groups

Small groups are what nurture the international congregation. Church leadership should see themselves in some way as a small group, giving nurture and development to one another. There are various types of groups:

- New people
- Non-Christians
- Special needs
- Counseling
- Young mothers dealing with pressures of raising children in a cross-cultural situation
- Older women who are international wives of nationals.

Group duties include:

- Hospitality (ushers and greeters)
- Fellowship
- Internet coordinator
- Special services team
- Evangelism and international outreach team

Invitations to speak at local universities and public schools can also be considered as ministry opportunities. The impact of this message in English has a lasting effect on the children and can spark their curiosity to learn more about Christian values.

15. Attending and Worshiping in the Korean Church

As co-laborers with Korean pastors, worshiping and speaking to the Korean congregation in the church service with translation is encouraged. There were opportunities to:

- Exchange ideas and programs with other English worship ministries, including music, Sunday School material for kids, evangelism, and outreach to the men of the sea on the large ocean ships that came into the harbor.
- Be co-laborers with their missionaries.

16. Missionary Centers

Traditionally, overseas missionaries and mission boards have developed missionary centers for their international people.

- The missionaries did church planting
- Conducted services at the local Korean churches
- Taught many subjects at the local Korean seminary.

17. Church Planting for Evangelism

Church planting movements are going on all over the world, and hundreds and thousands of souls are coming to know Christ as their personal Savior. Much prayer is behind these church planting movements. Prayer provides opportunities in the missionary's personal life for reaching people and leads to the life of the new church and its leaders.

A church planting movement emerges where:

- Evangelism is abundant
- Sowing of the Gospel is abundant
- A plan was implemented for a church planting

18. Establishing Christian Education for the Children of Leaders

It is important to establish Christian Education for the children of pastors, international professors and missionaries. Teaching children on the mission field is a great opportunity to teach them to be fruitful disciples of Jesus Christ. They will be exposed to different cultures and have a chance to learn firsthand how people outside the West actually live. Ministry opportunities include:

- Teaching
- Conducting chapel programs
- Developing Christian curriculum
- Fulfilling administrative duties
- Working with the students and parents
- Establishing outreach in the local communities

For the veteran missionary, retirement is the main reason for leaving the mission field. The primary reason why younger to middle-aged families leave the field is the needs of the children of missionary families. Children also need to know how to handle culture shock. Educational options to choose from include:

- Homeschooling
- Online learning
- Local schools in the host country
- International Christian School

19. Planting an International School

The benefit of establishing an International Christian school include:

- Teachers will have the opportunity to learn a new language, experience a new culture, expand their own world view, as well as challenge and educate children from all over the world.
- Teachers are educators, mentors, disciplers, evangelists, and friends.
- Students will be given a biblically integrated curriculum with prayer.

Prayer Points:

1. Pray for the daily leading of the Spirit in your life. Pray for wisdom, direction and favor in all areas of your life that God's perfect peace reign and rule in your life.

2. Pray about an area of ministry that you may want to get involved in internationally.

3. Pray for and with church plants in an international country of interest.

4. Pray for teachers in international Christian schools that they excel in their field of study, evangelism to students and impact upon the international communities.

Personal Devotion:

Write a brief devotion on God's faithfulness in our lives as he leads and guides us into his perfect will and direction for our lives. This devotion should be 100-150 words.

Discussion Points:

1. Discuss what it means to be led by the Spirit. Give examples in your own personal life? Respond in 100-150 words.

2. Use scripture as a foundation and points within this chapter and discuss a biblical model of church planting. Respond in 100-150 words.

3. Discuss ways and methods to protect and guide children during times of ministry transition. If possible, offer personal examples. Respond in 100-150 words.

Reflection and Application Essay:

International ministries provide Christian teaching ministry opportunities. From the list mentioned in the chapter, identify one that would be of interest and then identify the ministry and who is the target audience, what you would do and outline potential steps of success. Your paper should be 3-pages using MLA, APA or Turabian formatting.

Chapter 6

Cultural Adaptation

Key Concepts and Learning Objectives

1. Personal Identity and Social Identity

In a foreign country, missionaries must learn to interact effectively with people from the local culture (and with other missionaries) to be effective. People who serve abroad must become integrated into:

- A whole new country
- The physical environment
- The community
- The people
- The new ministry or position

Missionaries must learn how to interact in the culture in which they wish to communicate. For the Christian message to be heard, it must be communicated *slowly, clearly and simply*. Differences within cultures must be taken into account. Personal and social identity come together when the cultural differences are minimized, possibly overlooked, and a mutual trust with all people is established.

2. Language Barrier, Culture Shock, and Discouragement

Language is a major component to bridging the gaps between cultures. Learning the language is clearly essential in adapting to the host culture.

- Those who have short-term assignments do not need to be fluent in the language, but they should learn many phrases to survive.

- Those who plan to stay longer should learn the language for communication purposes and to show that one cares enough about the Nationals to make the effort.

- Most Nationals are studying English, but rarely do they know English well-enough to understand spiritual matters.

- Internationals want to communicate spiritually; they must speak slowly or have an interpreter for translation.

- The mother tongue receives and comprehends spiritual truth.

3. Culture Shock

Culture shock has been defined as a special kind of anxiety with uneasiness, a sense of disorientation where individuals no longer feel in control, and a stressful experience by people who enter a culture radically different from their own. International people must learn to do things differently: *working, eating, talking and living.* Culture shock produces a number of symptoms which all people living abroad need to be aware of: fatigue, discomfort, generalized frustration, a feeling of helplessness, the inability to cope with the demands of the day, excessive preoccupation with personal cleanliness, concerns about food, pure drinking water, excessive washing of hands, personal health, minor pains, and skin rashes. Fear of physical contact with attendants, excessive fear of being cheated, robbed, or injured result in negative feelings toward hosts, refusal to learn their language or practice their common courtesies, irritability at slight annoyances, criticisms, and delays are other minor frustrations, loneliness, a need to meet others, (but a reluctance to let them see our emotional state), a longing for home, for emails, for home cooking, and good TV programs are other emotional frustrations, loss of inventiveness, naturalness, and flexibility so that work declines in quality, and difficulty in communicating feelings to others result from these frustrations. (See pages 100-101 in book for complete list)

The most common causes of culture shock may be found in situational factors. (See pages 101-102 in book for complete list.)

4. Overcoming Cultural Shock

Culture shock can contribute to personal growth. It is a positive experience in character building, deepening faith, and increasing motivation to learn and to adapt. Culture shock can be overcome or mitigated by:

- Taking a personal interest in others, moving the focus away from themselves and their problems.
- Surrounding themselves with familiar things.
- Slowing down, simplifying daily tasks, relaxing, and letting emotions catch up with the new culture.
- Developing specific patterns and following the same routine each day to get a sense of familiarity.
- Giving expression to their feelings by crying, laughing, singing, praying, or drawing a picture to ease the stress and anxiety.
- Revising their goals, instead of blaming themselves for failures, giving new energy to language study and using it for simple occasions.
- Finding times and places to get physical exercise.
- Making a few small decisions, and carrying them out to build confidence.

Pray for God's grace and tolerance. The struggles they faced are not only cultural, but also spiritual. Determine to adapt to the Nationals, develop a positive attitude, and look for the many good things in the foreign culture.

5. Discouragement on the Foreign Field

Some newcomers to the foreign field go through periods of discouragement. Discouragement is a tool of the devil. When down, get back up quickly—the quicker the better. Adjusting rapidly to the new culture and foreign people is extremely important. There are several things internationals can do to overcome discouragement:

- Maintain a positive attitude.
- Pray.
- Receive comfort from Scripture.
- Put mind over matter.
- Have a willingness to serve God.
- Keep the mind off of trivial things, such as, cultural differences, crowded streets, and food preference differences.

Things that Nationals sometimes do that cause distress are:

- Not being on time
- Breaking their word or promise
- Lack of efficiency
- Change of schedules
- Leaving internationals out of conversations, ignoring them and causing them to feel unappreciated.

6. Homesickness and Loneliness

Some measures to overcome homesickness and loneliness are to call home, use email and the computer, and send text messages. See pages 105-106 for complete list.

7. Irritation and Frustration

People respond in various ways to the change in environment when they go overseas. There are some people who resist involvement in the local culture. Other people may reject their own home culture. Biblical examples of people reacting to a new culture include:

- Abraham, Gen. 12:10-13, 20:11-13
- Moses, Ex. 4:24-26
- Jonah, Jonah 4

Frustrations come from different situations, and they have to be dealt with. Some common frustrations are:

- A sense of insignificance
- Powerlessness

8. Coping, Adapting and Minimizing Cultural Differences

There is no place for carelessness, quitting or wavering in God's service. Patience is a fundamental requirement and is frequently in short supply. A healthy approach to understanding and managing conflict is vital for cross-cultural relationships. To enjoy the host culture, international people must:

- Reach out.
- Make friends.
- Adapt to their new environment as quickly as possible.
- Keep an open mind about the differences in cultures, ways of doing things, and values.
- Have forgiving hearts and ask God to help them to accept and to cope with the new situations and with the people.
- All criticism should be avoided.
- Keep a positive and Christ-like attitude.
- Remember their calling to go and serve the people of all nations.

Entering into another culture means enjoying and respecting that culture and participating in it. Missionaries are not called to adopt the host culture, but to adapt to it. Internationals who try to integrate too much, too, fast, usually experience conflict with other Internationals and people in the host culture. International people must reach out in humility, in respect, in friendliness, in God's love, without giving up their own habits and culture. Do not try to just cope in a foreign culture, but:

- Try to overlook and overcome the new culture.
- Learn different ways of doing things.
- Get used to the things that were initial culture shock.

9. Enjoying God's Assignment

Struggles abroad are not only cultural, but also spiritual. Internationals must reflect a positive attitude and see things in a new way. Look for good things in a foreign culture; there are many.

- Discover new food
- Go out of our way to make a circle of friends
- Cultivate a positive attitude of exploration and adventure

A balance must be established with international and national people; otherwise, isolation from the natives that must be served may result. Relationships with other missionaries should not hinder the real need to adapt and develop contacts with Nationals.

10. Cultural Sensitivity

The key to cultural sensitivity lies in the ability of a person to be aware of, understand, and respond positively to the cultural diversity of nationals within the host culture. It is important to become acquainted with the cultural heritage of the Nationals, including the culture of their backgrounds to attain a better understanding of who they are now. The Gospel is a transcultural Gospel, and Jesus demonstrated a culturally sensitive attitude toward those to whom He ministered.

Check our own sensitivity to the country culture where we are living by:

- Learning the culture
- Finding a mentor and national life coach from the host culture to help develop a deeper appreciation for the culture
- Avoiding making cultural slurs or derogatory connotations about the people, the country, or the system

- Using proper personal names of people and the current names of countries

11. Misconceptions That May Stifle Your Ministry

It becomes easier to serve God when three underlying misconceptions are given up. The three misconceptions are:

- The first misconception is that we are going there to help the people. When we see only the need in others and not the need in ourselves, this approach is bound to fail.
- The second misconception is that we may think that we are the only one doing anything.
- The third misconception is when we think that our gifts will be fully used. Coming from a developed country, we often think that the gifts we bring will surely be wanted, needed and used.

As we reach out to others in love, our sole expectation should be our own simple obedience.

12. Obstacles Serving Abroad: God's Grace Is Sufficient

As a result of inconveniences, cultural differences and hardships, some missionaries withdraw and go back to their home culture. Here are a few of the obstacles:

- The country and the people are not as they had expected.
- Maybe there is inadequate heating, and fuel oil is used instead of gas or electric.
- The food is very different, and there is very little western food to buy.
- Transportation is inconvenient, subways and buses are overcrowded, and the streets are very crowded with many traffic jams.

- Other international missionaries are not easy to get along with; nationals may be wary of us and may not connect with us.

- Issues of sickness, fungus, mosquito bites, and stomach problems arise because of different food.

- Local doctors may not want to treat the illnesses of Internationals because of a communication problem or lack of understanding the problems or symptoms.

Circumstances may or may not hinder our ministry, but sinful attitudes certainly will. Internationals living abroad must have a mindset to cope, adjust, and make friends with nationals, and go forward with the purpose and plan for their ministry with the Grace of God and His hands of blessings on their lives.

Prayer Points:

1. Pray for missionaries in your church or that you know that they adapt to their host culture in healthy way for fruitful ministry.

2. Pray for understanding and opportunities to dialogue and witness to people of diverse cultures.

3. Pray and declare encouragement over missionaries in your church or that you know to defeat discouragement.

4. Pray for joy and contentment in your current professional and/or ministry platform knowing that all things work together for good to those who love him and are called according to his purpose.

Personal Devotion:

Write a brief devotion using scripture to encourage a missionary who is dealing with discouragement and homesickness. This devotion should be 100-150 words.

A Study Guide for Preparing for the International Harvest

Discussion Points:

1. Missionaries must learn how to interact in the culture in which they wish to communicate. Give two examples of the Apostle Paul doing this. How effective was he? Respond in 100-150 words.

2. Give a personal example of your experience with culture shock and how you dealt with it. Respond in 100-150 words.

3. Discuss an occurrence in a ministry setting where your expectations did not match reality. How did you respond and deal with it? Respond in 100-150 words.

Reflection and Application Essay:

Research your country or location of ministry and identify at least five cultural differences and how you would overcome those cultural differences. Part 2, identify 3-5 areas of cultural sensitivity that you would have to beware of as a result of being immersed in Western culture. Your paper should be 3-pages using MLA, APA or Turabian formatting.

Chapter 7

Serving Internationally: A Major Commitment

Key Concepts and Learning Objectives

1. Serving Internationally — A Life-changing Experience

God can be properly revealed only through diversity. To fully understand God's creation of diversity among people requires learning and understanding which are incompatible with egocentrism and superiority. We are called to love all people. The more authentic relationships that are made, the greater the ability to communicate God's truth.

2. Lack of Readiness — Unprepared to Serve Effectively

Lack of readiness is one of the biggest obstacles of God's people, including missionaries, who are called abroad to serve. You should have these things ready before you go:

- Internationals should have a well-developed skill or profession to take with them.
- Go through training and orientation programs, and complete courses at a Christian college.
- Get acquainted with the country and culture.

Whatever the missionary does, it should be done with excellence. When people go to the host country, they learn that the Nationals are not as backward as they thought. Anyone who is called to go abroad should get proper training to be prepared for God's ministry and service. Training for overseas experiences should:

- Increase learning ability
- Make people more understanding, adaptable and flexible
- Improve foreign language skills
- Deepen the overall spiritual life and relationship with God.

For Internationals to be effective, they must:

- Develop interpersonal skills to be better communicators.
- Be knowledgeable in the Word.
- Know how to effectively teach and communicate it.
- Hear the Word, worship, have fellowship, and attend Bible studies.

3. Training, Education and Qualities for Servanthood

Good practical training with relevant experiences beforehand is necessary to gain confidence when going overseas. Preparedness will also promote more self-confidence in communicating with Nationals.

Internationals should:

- Pray.
- Accept the opportunities God brings to them without feeling they are too good or too qualified to do menial things for God and His people.
- Develop a servant's heart and be willing to do whatever it takes to reach the people for Christ.
- Develop the ability to get along with people.
- Not do things in the flesh, for self-glory, or to enhance their credentials, but to keep the primary focus on God and doing things for Him, seeking every opportunity that He puts before them.
- Have compassion and overlook the weaknesses of all people, even when it adversely affects us.

Missionary training provides opportunities for meeting people with different backgrounds and provides practical opportunities to witness and to lead people to Christ.

4. Qualities of a Missionary

Serving abroad is a major undertaking and requires a total commitment. Every Christian needs to develop the following qualities, especially missionaries:

- Insight or spiritual discernment
- Adaptability along with flexibility and versatility
- Perseverance
- Zeal for sharing the gospel
- Ability to get along with others
- Emotional stability
- Humility
- Spiritual maturity
- A Spirit-filled life

5. Characteristics of a Missionary

The Christians' first responsibility as missionaries is to offer themselves. 10 characteristics that every successful missionary should have developed before going on an overseas assignment:

- Dedication
- Spirituality
- Faith and trust
- Love
- Conviction
- Purpose
- Discernment
- Enthusiasm
- Perseverance
- Leadership

6. Ongoing Training and Development

Some missionaries, after a time in the field, begin to recognize deficiencies in their own educational backgrounds. Often missionaries take extended furloughs, so they can complete the education and training needed, while reconnecting with their local church before returning to the field.

Greater needs of the missionary compared to the domestic worker are:

- Adapt to another language.
- Adapt to another culture.
- Adapt to other living standards.
- Adapt to a lack of equipment, and they must do without many conveniences we take for granted at home.

7. Missionary Work as a Spiritual Service Rendered to God

Missionary work is first of all a spiritual service rendered to God, because of His calling on the life of the individual. There can never be any satisfactory substitute for a real, personal knowledge and experience with Christ. No amount of education can take the place of this personal relationship.

Missionaries must:

- Have a heart for God.
- Be focused on God.
- Not be focused on self or worldly pleasures.

8. Prepare, Then Go Serve

Missionaries must be prepared to present the Gospel, and to seek to change the course and objectives of men's thinking. Missionary education should be:

- Preparation for living
- Preparation for service
- Preparation in broad cultural education and Bible training

(For additional information, read textbook pages 144-145 on missionary personality attributes by Harold Cook.)

9. Spiritual Gifts and Fruit of the Spirit

God expects Internationals to have a compassion for reaching the lost and to have strong, godly character. In turn, He will bless richly and abundantly, and will provide daily guidance and opportunities for ministry.

10. Preparation: Managing Loose Ends

Some things to consider are prior to leaving:

- Completion of current church ministries. Blessing by pastors and people of God.
- Blessings/approval by the immediate family.
- Storage of house furnishings and costs.
- Payments for life and health insurance.
- Filing of taxes, drivers' license renewals.
- Forwarding costs and procedures of mail.
- College tuition loan payments.
- Unfinished college degree programs.
- Boyfriend/girlfriend relationships.
- Friends and family members who plan to marry.
- Strategic anniversaries and weddings coming up.
- Parents and family members in ill health.
- Physician and health care follow up.

11. Suffering Produces Rewards

Whether we are missionaries or businessmen, we all suffer to a certain degree. Suffering is part of living and is to be expected. This is especially true for those who are called to reach unreached people of the world. The excessive amount of suffering of the Apostle Paul is unimaginable. As described in the MEV, 2 Cor. 11:23-28, we get a clear picture of the cumulative pain and sorrow of Paul's missionary life: pain multiplied upon pain, beaten the second time on the same back, opening all the scars, some months later happening a third time. By enduring suffering with patience, the reward of our experience of God's glory in heaven increases.

- Paul said, "For the light and momentary troubles are achieving for us an eternal glory that far outweighs them all. So, we fix our eyes not on what is seen, but on what is unseen. For what is seen is temporary, but what is unseen is eternal." 2 Cor 4:17-18.
- Jesus said, "Blessed are you when men revile you and persecute you and say all kinds of evil against you falsely on my account. Rejoice and be glad for your reward is great in heaven." Matthew 5:11-12.

God will use the suffering of his devoted servants to wake people and motivate them to take risks for God.

12. Reaching People for Christ

Paul's sufferings were the means God was using to bring salvation to the Corinthian church. They could see the suffering love of Christ in Paul. He was actually sharing in Christ's sufferings and making them real for the church. Christ is calling His church to world missions. He has made it clear that one must suffer for the cause of salvation and coming to Christ. *(See textbook pages 152-153, the positive side of missionary suffering by John Piper.)* Joy in suffering brings forth hope in a great reward. Christians are not called to live lives of burdensome persecution but are called to rejoice.

The goal of missions is that people from all nations worship the true God and treasure the preciousness of God above all else including life itself. Missionaries are sent out to break strongholds among the nations and bring hope in God.

The way of love is:

- The way of self-denial
- The way of ultimate joy when the believer puts his hope in God
- The way of greatest good to others

Prayer Points:

1. Pray for God to reveal to you the qualities of a missionary that you need to address and focus on.

2. Pray for missionaries that you know as well as yourself that they are completely prepared to embark on God's missionary plan for their life.

3. Pray that your heart always stays pliable to God's heart and compassionate to the people you are sent to.

4. Pray for a revival for Christian missionaries that an awakening happens for unbelievers in their assigned countries.

Personal Devotion:

Identify a biblical Character and show how they were lacking in areas for their calling. How did God then prepare them to make sure they were ready? This devotion should be 100-150 words.

Discussion Points:

1. In this chapter of study items are mentioned to be effective for international ministry. Identify the two strongest for you and weakest for you and why? Respond in 100-150 words.

2. What is biblical suffering and how does God use it. Have you gone through a period of suffering and what was the result? Respond in 100-150 words.

3. Identify the nine gifts of the spirit and how they function. Which one are you most proficient with? Respond in 100-150 words.

Reflection and Application Essay:

For this assignment you are putting together a "TO DO" list of at least 10 things you must have done prior to leaving for a year-long missions' trip. Identity the list and how you will accomplish each item. Your paper should be 2-3-pages using MLA, APA or Turabian formatting.

Chapter 8

Fulfilling the Great Commission — God's Command

Key Concepts and Learning Objectives

1. Fulfill Your Calling — Go, Serve, and Make Disciples of All Nations

Matthew 28:18-19, The Great Commission, the command is to:

- Go. The commission is to *"go,"* and the extent is *"into all the world."* As we go, we are to announce the good news of the Gospel to every creature.

- Require Repentance. Repentance is part of the message of the Great Commission. In Luke 24:47, remission of sins is an integral part of the message of the Great Commission. The word for *remission* includes freedom, pardon, deliverance, forgiveness, and liberty.

We are sent into the world to fulfill the same mission that Jesus came to fulfill. Every Christian is called to be a global disciple in the sense that we are witnesses to what God has done in our lives. Wherever we go, we are disciples in our careers:

- Full time missions or church related service
- Banking
- Education
- Medicine
- Management

- Law
- Business
- Etc....

The first formal missionary outreach began in Antioch. North American Christians can trace their spiritual origins to the missionary movement initiated in Antioch.

2. The Mission from God

It is imperative to spend the time and energy to be fully trained, getting the education, a good spiritual foundation, and cross-cultural preparation to enhance one's self as a person called by God to fulfill His purpose of building and expanding the Kingdom of God. that over two billion have never personally heard about Jesus Christ. The Great Commission says that we are to make disciples of all nations or people groups.

- Evangelize all people.
- Establish churches to carry on God's work.
- The Gospel will be spread throughout the land.

What can we learn from the planting of the faith in Antioch? How was it won for Christ? It was won by a spontaneous movement of a handful of wandering Christians moving up the coast from Jerusalem. God uses ordinary people to carry out His commission as He did in the Antioch church; however, we must be willing to be used. The result in Antioch was:

- The conversion of a great number of individuals.
- Established a Biblical church.
- The church was nurtured by Barnabas who encouraged them in their spiritual growth.
- Barnabas and Paul met with the church and taught great numbers of people.
- Disciples were called Christians first at Antioch.

- The church contributed to a relief effort during a period of famine in another land.
- Antioch became the mission base for world evangelism.
- The Antioch missionaries followed instructions to plant churches cross-culturally.
- There was diversity in the first missionary church, as God intended for Christ's body, but there was unity during the diversity.
- The ability of the leadership of this church was able to connect and serve together.
- The Antioch Church demonstrated how to be effective in God's service in diversity, unity, solid theology, and demonstration of spirituality.

Discipleship training in preparation for missions work like Antioch should include:

- Basic understanding of the structure and general content of the books of the Bible.
- Prayer
- Salvation
- Assurance
- Guidance
- The church
- Evangelism

3. Not What We Had Expected: Lack of Full Preparation

God was preparing us to serve internationally. We were prepared both academically with advanced degrees and spiritually, serving in the church for several years. Our commitment was full time service to the Lord. We lacked:

- Preparation in language acquisition

- Expectations
- Cultural diversity
- Knowledge of food and customs
- Survival in a foreign country

Our goal coming to South Korea was to use our God-given skills in providing Christian education and ministering to the people. We arrived, feeling out of place, helpless, and upset. Everything was different, and the ways of doing things were not what we had ever experienced. The issues were more complex than we had imagined! We felt inadequate to be able to make an impact in the culture and society, because we did not know how to live and get around and were not fully informed. International missionaries encouraged us to focus on the goal of adapting and doing our ministry. We were not prepared enough to cope with the culture shock.

4. Cross-Cultural Perspectives

Our view of God was greatly enhanced as we learned to trust Him completely. When meeting people from a different culture and sharing our lives, we discovered that God is greater than either of our cultures. Cross-cultural travel and relationships have expanded our view of God:

- God speaks every language.
- Cross-cultural worship services have made us realize that He really is "Lord of all the nations."
- Hearing the testimonies of other Christians has given us a new view of the good news of Jesus Christ.
- Ministering cross-culturally has changed our view of God and who He is.

We could describe our personal transformation in these terms:

- We discovered that we could live comfortably and happily with fewer material things.

- Although we had more material possessions in America, it seemed our faith was not as deep as that of the Korean Christians.

- Our perspective on hardship changed.

- Our understanding of the creative diversity of God is enlarged.

- Worshipping with Korean Christians has challenged our fervor in prayer and our anticipation of heavenly worship, praise and adoration of Jesus Christ.

- Cross-cultural services and worship give us a little taste of heavenly worship.

5. God's Provision

Traveling abroad and throughout the country of Korea, we relied on God for safety and He took care of us every step of the way. Our faith was stretched to higher levels. Unpredictable situations, unfamiliar foods and ministering in areas in which we did not feel confident, challenged us to depend on God instead of ourselves.

6. Maintaining Spiritual Effectiveness

Living in Korea helped us to be away from the distractions and materialism of our home country. Teaming up with other International people with a spiritual focus in a new culture helped us to grow to new spiritual levels. This is due to:

- Intense focus on the spiritual
- Dependency
- Understanding
- Applying spiritual truths as revealed by God through prayer
- Bible studies
- Spiritual interaction
- Evangelism and integration into daily living.

From our experiences on the field, these are some areas where missionaries and tentmakers can maintain a spiritual focus and to minister effectively:

- Devotions
- Church attendance and fellowship
- Testimonies
- Sharing the Gospel
- Presenting the Gospel
- Prayer teams
- Time with God
- Bible studies

People who are called to the mission field to minister must stay focused on planning, prioritizing and seeking opportunities for their spiritual growth. Spiritual giving, servanthood, growth and enhancement will provide ministry opportunities and momentum to continue serving abroad.

Prayer Points:

1. Pray for God to give you clarity on your specific area of ministry and to take advantage of missional opportunities every day.

2. Pray for missionaries, future missionaries and/or yourself for awareness and strength to acclimate to the native culture of ministry.

3. Pray for continual means and methods for ministry preparation for your future endeavors.

4. Pray for God's provision and spiritual effectiveness for yourself and missionaries you know to accomplish the plan and purpose of God.

Personal Devotion:

Identify three qualities about the Antioch Church that has caught your attention. Why does it interest you and how can you use those qualities today? This devotion should be 100-150 words.

Discussion Points:

1. What are the key aspects of the Great Commission? Give examples of these aspects today. Respond in 100-150 words.

2. What does it mean to be a global disciple? Give an example in your life? Respond in 100-150 words.

3. What does "cross-cultural" perspectives mean? Give a personal example. Respond in 100-150 words.

Reflection and Application Essay:

Maintaining spiritual effectiveness is crucial for missional success. Identify 5 areas or practices that you will intentionally put into practice to stay spiritually effective in diverse cultures. Identify the practices, why they are important to you, give scriptural foundation and an action plan. Your paper should be 3-pages using MLA, APA or Turabian formatting.

Chapter 9

Getting Started in Ministry

Key Concepts and Learning Objectives

1. Getting Started in Ministry

Pursuing international ministry and missions requires obedience to a God-given spiritual journey. The more planning and preparation, the greater will be the spiritual impact of the mission abroad.

- Equip yourself spiritually.
- Serve in your local church.
- Receive an academic education.
- Establish relationships with people from other cultures.
- Become aware of options for going overseas with continued preparation (missions agencies).
- Discern His specific plan for your life with continued training and development. (Know your specific calling.)

2. Preparing to be a Global Christian Disciple

Becoming an effective global disciple requires time and is a continuing work in process in preparation for missions and ministry. The processes include:

- Education
- Hands on practical ministry
- Mentoring

On-the-job mentoring will provide a higher success rate with improved results and learning as you grow will develop you into a more fully effective missionary for Christ. It will also complement and build on the earlier training, education, and development that you had with your pastor(s), churches, and in traveling abroad. Continuous learning includes reading, self-study with personal development and improvement goals according to your specific ministry. Secrets of a successful ministry include:

- Prayer with a right relationship with God and pure motives.
- Be a mentor and remodel in the faith.
- Continuous personal development.

Kingdom work is about:

- Servanthood
- Dedication and commitment
- Giving to others

3. Nurturing Christians to Serve

Planning for any ministry responsibility requires leadership. The church pastor should be equipped, concerning missions and ministry, to teach three basic lessons to the church.

- Scriptures present missions and ministry as an essential teaching in the church, and not as an extra program.
- The church will receive great blessings from taking part in the work.
- The church must have an important role in the missionary work of the Lord.

The church is the natural recruiting ground for Christian people being called into ministry. The church is a place where young Christians become interested in Christianity and are nurtured in the work and service of the Lord. Preparation and training will be a time to ensure their calling is real and genuine, Christians must:

- Be dedicated whole-heartedly to Christ
- Be dedicated to ministry and missions

- Be challenged to look at the world's needs and their own possibilities, taking inventory of the gifts and skills that have been given to them.
- Be prepared for whatever God has for them.

4. Nurturing Christians in Missions

Training must emphasize the motives and purpose of missions and ministry - including God's calling. Attitude is very important on the mission field. Those who are called abroad to be global disciples should display a kind and loving spirit despite many unfavorable circumstances they may encounter. How churches can help:

- Churches may invite missionaries to speak.
- Provide opportunities for Christians to meet and talk to missionaries personally. A discussion group or a small gathering in a home for a personal contact with people serving abroad will be invaluable for church members interested in missions.

5. Training in the Church

The church should not provide a separate missions and ministry training program from its regular education and training programs. Everyone is an ambassador for Christ. Specialized training must be done at a training school to prepare for missions' work. The church can and should offer:

- Foundational training for the people to be good witnesses for Christ everywhere.
- Christian growth in personal dedication and the spiritual life.
- Christians must learn how to put "the kingdom of God and His righteousness" first in their lives.
- Training in systematic Bible studies.
- Training in personal witnessing, outreach and evangelism.
- Leadership and service opportunities

Church leaders who have a heart for missions can direct missionary candidates to schools and courses in education and training that will best meet their needs.

Prayer Points:

1. Pray for areas in your local church to serve and grow.

2. Pray for a school to attend for Biblical academic training and preparation.

3. Pray for a deeper relationship with the Lord resulting in pure heart motives.

4. Pray for ways your local church can continue and improve upon preparing and engaging missionaries.

Personal Devotion:

Are there any areas in your life that God does not have control of or maybe you have not surrendered to him? What steps will you to take to dedicate those areas to him? This devotion should be 100-150 words.

Discussion Points:

1. What does biblical mentoring look like and what should it accomplish? Respond in 100-150 words.

2. What should Kingdom work be about? Give an example in your life? Respond in 100-150 words.

3. What does it mean in your opinion that training in the local church must emphasize the motives and purpose of missions and ministry Respond in 100-150 words.

Reflection and Application Essay:

It has been said in this chapter that the more planning and preparation, the greater will be the spiritual impact of the mission abroad. For this reflection and application, have a conversation with someone from another culture. What were some of the differences that you each had? Was there any barrier with language? What are some areas that you need to work on with cultural diversity to enhance those types of conversations and engagements? Explain the culture of the person and background and then respond to the questions asked for the paper in ample detail. Your paper should be 3-pages using MLA, APA or Turabian formatting.

Chapter 10

The Purpose of a Prayerful Life

Key Concepts and Learning Objectives

1. Prayerful Life is Essential for Christian Living

When Jesus looked out at the mission field, He instructed His disciples in ways to pray. *"Ask the Lord of the harvest," (MEV, Matthew 9:38)* Workers are necessary, or; their work is necessary, but before anything else, comes prayer. Not all Christian people are called to the mission field; some are called to pray. A person can pray privately for some aspect of missions, but prayer should be informed, persistent and expectant, just like the persistent widow in Luke 18:3. Leaders in missions are:

- Often the quickest to admit their need of prayer
- The greatest believers in its power

The church must take proactive measures to provide prayer support for those who are called overseas to minister. Prayer:

- Sustains the missionary and international ministry workers
- Breaks the strongholds of Satan
- Prevents many obstacles
- Reinforces the mission and ministry
- Removes roadblocks
- Keeps a person uplifted

- Fights the opposition
- Affects change
- Lessens spiritual warfare
- Provides added blessings
- Provides encouragement
- Meets the needs of the international people

2. Supporting with Prayer

Missionaries have a great need for the prayers from the church, its pastors and from those people at home who know how to pray effectively. We must be very diligent in our prayers and ask Him for the nations which have yet to be evangelized. Prayer is important in knowing and doing God's will daily.

- Psalm 2:8
- Psalm 119:26-48

3. Intercessory Prayer Needed

On the mission field, missionaries are called to present the Gospel and win souls for Christ. Sometimes they feel they are forgotten back home and can feel when the church is praying and when they are not praying. When obstacles and circumstances become overwhelming for the missionary, communications must be sent quickly to get people back home to increase their level of prayer support.

4. Prayer is the Responsibility of the Church

At home, the church has the awesome responsibility of praying for its missionaries and people serving overseas, so they can effectively do what they are called to do.

Some basic ideas for prayer are as follows:

- Pray regularly — do not wait for a catastrophe for inspiration to pray.
- Be persistent and persevere in prayer — missionaries are doing a work commanded by Christ. The Enemy will do all he can to stop it.
- Be specific in prayer — contact and ask the missionaries for whom you are praying what their needs are.
- Try to anticipate the needs of the missionaries — think of spiritual problems that God's servants living overseas may experience:
    o Time for reading and studying
    o Refreshment in prayer and Bible teaching
    o Humility and freedom from the temptation of pride
    o Wisdom in relations with other missionaries
    o Victory over irritation, criticism and cultural differences
    o Strength to overcome loneliness
    o A healthy outlook through difficulties while serving abroad

The call of Jesus is for prevailing prayer. The power of prayer is the weapon by which the nations will be brought to faith and obedience for the glory of God. People serving overseas must present their needs and requests in a way that people back home will pray individually and regularly in:

- Prayer meetings
- Church services (The pastor should make missionary announcements in church services.)
- Sunday school classes
- Small groups

Christians who have accepted the Lord as their Savior have the responsibility of being ambassadors for Christ by:

- Praying regularly
- Using personal spiritual gifts to win souls and to further the work for the Kingdom of Christ at home and internationally

Prayer Points:

1. Pray that you will experience many life changes as you faithfully serve God and you will be fully prepared and equipped for service in His Kingdom.

2. Pray for overall needs of missionaries associated with your church or that you may know.

3. Pray for your church to get a greater desire for intercessory and prevailing prayer.

4. Pray for the salvation of souls in missionary represented countries.

Personal Devotion:

I Thessalonians 5:16-18 instructs us to pray without ceasing. First, what does this mean in context and how can you make it applicable to your Spiritual formation? This devotion should be 100-150 words.

Discussion Points:

1. From the chapter, a person can pray privately for some aspect of missions, but prayer should be informed, persistent and expectant, just like the persistent widow in Luke 18:3. How is prayer informed, persistent and expectant? Respond in 100-150 words.

2. Explain how Psalms 2:8 is a textual example of supporting with prayer. Give an example of supporting prayer in your life. Respond in 100-150 words.

3. Describe 3-5 ways that technology could be incorporated as a tool to enhance prayer in the church and intercessory prayer. Respond in 100-150 words.

Reflection and Application Essay:

Staying within the idea of The Purpose of a Prayerful Life, 1) explain the fundamental idea of the concept, 2) Identify 3 scriptural passages that deal with a prayerful life and how? Lastly, identify and explain 3-5 personal things you can do to make prayer more intentional and purposeful in your life. Your paper should be 3-pages using MLA, APA or Turabian formatting.

Chapter 11

Conclusion

Key Concepts and Learning Objectives

Mastering the Call of God

Mastering God's call takes some attitude adjustment on our part. We cannot expect to "do what we have always done and in the way we have always done it." It's important to go into a new environment trying to adjust in ways of life there.

- Allow God to guide and direct each step. for you. Be patient.
- Be flexible and anticipate change each day.

The keys to mastering the call of God are:

- Language. Learning the language will be a tremendous benefit. An everlasting impact will be made by speaking the host language.
- Expectation. The smallest tasks may take a great amount of time. Never expect to accomplish multiple tasks on the "to do" list. Do not feel that tasks must be done now. Expectations must be lowered, allowing God to be in control of the ministry.
- Building Relationship. Some missionaries tend to isolate themselves and need encouragement to get away. Developing friendships cross-culturally takes time and effort.
- Forgiveness. Missionaries and God's people called abroad may not provide encouraging support for each other, as they may be

struggling themselves. At times, people may not act as Christians should, and it is hard to cope when we experience conflicts with other Christians. This is a major problem living abroad.

- Communications. Newsletters and emails to family, friends, church members, pastors and mentors should be done quickly and regularly, especially if immediate prayer support is required.

- Expanding Your World View into Global Thinking. Most advice about living abroad applies to cross-cultural people, global disciples, regardless of their calling and purpose for being overseas. Being a God-called missionary, we could equip the people to carry out God's plan and purpose, not only locally, but to other parts of the world.

- When Jesus told us to go into all the world and preach the Gospel to every creature, it gave us comfort to know that He would always be with us. *"For God is not unrighteous to forget your work and labour of love, which you have shewed toward His name, in that you have ministered to the saints, and do minister."* (MEV, Hebrews 6:10)

Prayer Points:

1. Pray for new and innovative ways to reach culture nationally and internationally.

2. Pray for opportunities to engage believers and non-believers for Kingdom expansion.

3. Pray for clear direction on your call for God and what the next step is.

4. Pray to the Holy Spirit to reveal, help, and heal any emotional or spiritual wounds.

Personal Devotion:

What does Philippians 2:5 have to say about attitudes? What does it mean to you personally? This devotion should be 100-150 words.

Discussion Points:

1. What does the Bible have to say about unforgiveness, give two scripture references? How can it impact you negatively? Have you ever carried unforgiveness and how did you deal with it? Respond in 100-150 words.

2. The chapter talks about expectations. What is meant by the author in lowering expectations? Have you ever been in a similar situation? Respond in 100-150 words.

3. After reading the entirety of the book what are three concepts from the content and/or the author's experience that you are going to put into active use and why? Respond in 100-150 words.

Reflection and Application Essay:

In this concluding essay the task at hand is to attempt to bring more closure and clarity to God's calling upon your life. Using three outside sources of your choosing in addition to the textbook, identify what the calling of God is in general on someone (not your calling). Considering this after reading the book where and to what do you believe God is calling you? What are 3-5 key areas from the book do you need to work on the most to prepare for that specific calling? Your paper should be 3-pages using MLA, APA or Turabian formatting.

Addendum

Chapter Scriptures

Each chapter of the book covers various topics to prepare missionaries for international Kingdom work. It is imperative for missionaries to stay encouraged and grounded in scripture. To aid in the study of the content of each chapter and to provide the life altering direction and promises from God's Word, scripture verses are associated with each chapter for the learner to memorize and mediate on for further preparation for ministry and personal devotion. The scriptures will also reinforce your prayer directives for each lesson. Scriptures are listed in the Modern English Version (MEV).

Chapter 1 — Introduction

- Isaiah 6:8, "Also I heard the voice of the Lord saying, "Whom shall I send, and who will go for us? "Then I said, "Here am I. Send me."

- Matthew 28:19, "Go therefore and make disciples of all nations, baptizing them in the name of the Father and of the Son and of the Holy Spirit."

Chapter 2 — The Emerging of an Upcoming Missionary

- John 4:35, "Do you not say, 'There are yet four months, and then comes the harvest'? Listen! I say to you, lift up your eyes and look at the fields, for they are already white for harvest."

- Acts 1:8, "But you shall receive power when the Holy Spirit comes upon you. And you shall be My witnesses in Jerusalem, and in all Judea and Samaria, and to the ends of the earth."

Chapter 3 — The International Church

- Matthew 5:13-16, "You are the salt of the earth. But if the salt loses its saltiness, how shall it be made salty? It is from then on good for nothing but to be thrown out and to be trampled underfoot by men.14 "You are the light of the world. A city that is set on a hill cannot be hidden. 15 Neither do men light a candle and put it under a basket, but on a candlestick. And it gives light to all who are in the house. 16 Let your light so shine before men that they may see your good works and glorify your Father who is in heaven."

- Romans 15:5-7, "Now may the God of perseverance and encouragement grant you to live in harmony with one another in accordance with Christ Jesus, 6 so that together you may with one voice glorify the God and Father of our Lord Jesus Christ. 7 Therefore welcome one another, just as Christ also welcomed us, for the glory of God."

Chapter 4 — The Challenge of Living in Foreign Environments

- I Peter 2:20-22, "For what credit is it if when you are being beaten for your sins you patiently endure? But if when doing good and suffering for it, you patiently endure, this is favorable before God. 21 For to this you were called, because Christ suffered for us, leaving us an example, that you should follow His steps:22 "He committed no sin, nor was deceit found in His mouth."

- Psalms 133, "Behold, how good and how pleasant it is for brothers to dwell together in unity!2 It is like precious oil upon the head, that runs down on the beard—even Aaron's beard— and going down to the collar of his garments; 3 as the dew of Hermon, that descends upon the mountains of Zion, for there the LORD has commanded the blessing, even life forever."

Chapter 5 — International Ministry Opportunities

- 2 Timothy 4:2, " Preach the word, be ready in season and out of season, reprove, rebuke, and exhort, with all patience and teaching."

- I Corinthians 9:19-23, "19 For though I am free from all men, I have made myself servant to all, that I might win even more. 20 To the Jews, I became as a Jew, that I might win the Jews; to those who are under the law, as under the law, that I might win those who are under the law; 21 to those who are outside the law, as outside the law (being not without God's law, but under Christ's law) that I might win those who are outside the law. 22 To the weak, I became as weak, that I might win the weak. I have become all things to all men, that I might by all means save some. 23 This I do for the gospel's sake, that I might partake of it with you."

Chapter 6 — Cultural Adaptation

- Psalms 37:7, "Rest in the LORD, and wait patiently for Him; do not fret because of those who prosper in their way, because of those who make wicked schemes."

- Matthew 25:40, "The King will answer, 'Truly I say to you, as you have done it for one of the least of these brothers of Mine, you have done it for Me.'"

Chapter 7 — Serving Internationally: A Major Commitment

- Galatians 5:22-23. "22 But the fruit of the Spirit is love, joy, peace, patience, gentleness, goodness, faith, 23 meekness, and self-control; against such there is no law."

- John 3:16, "For God so loved the world that He gave His only begotten Son, that whoever believes in Him should not perish, but have eternal life."

Chapter 8 — Fulfilling the Great Commission-God's Command

- 2 Peter 3:9, "The Lord is not slow concerning His promise, as some count slowness. But He is patient with us, because He does not want any to perish, but all to come to repentance."

- Acts 16:8-10, "8 So they passed by Mysia and went down to Troas. 9 During the night a vision appeared to Paul: A man of Macedonia stood and pleaded with him, saying, "Come over to Macedonia and help us." 10 After he had seen the vision, immediately we sought to go into Macedonia, concluding that the Lord had called us to preach the gospel to them.

Chapter 9 — Getting Started in Ministry

- Romans 12:1-2, "I urge you therefore, brothers, by the mercies of God, that you present your bodies as a living sacrifice, holy, and acceptable to God, which is your reasonable service of worship. 2 Do not be conformed to this world, but be transformed by the renewing of your mind, that you may prove what is the good and acceptable and perfect will of God."

- 2 Timothy 2:15, "Study to show yourself approved by God, a workman who need not be ashamed, rightly dividing the word of truth."

Chapter 10 — The Purpose of the Prayerful Life

- Matthew 9:36-39, "36 But when He saw the crowds, He was moved with compassion for them, because they fainted and were scattered, like sheep without a shepherd. 37 Then He said to His disciples, "The harvest truly is plentiful, but the laborers are few. 38 Therefore, pray to the Lord of the harvest, that He will send out laborers into His harvest."

- I Thessalonians 5:15-18, "16 Rejoice always. 17 Pray without ceasing. 18 In everything give thanks, for this is the will of God in Christ Jesus concerning you."

Chapter 11 — Conclusion

- Hebrews 6:9-11, "9 But though we speak in this manner, we are persuaded of better things for you, things that accompany salvation, 10 for God is not unjust so as to forget your work and labor of love that you have shown for His name, in that you have ministered to the saints and continue ministering. 11 We desire that every one of you show the same diligence for the full assurance of hope to the end,"

- Philippians 1:6, "I am confident of this very thing, that He who began a good work in you will perfect it until the day of Jesus Christ."

*The companion volume to this study guide,
Preparing for the International Harvest by Kenneth and Pauline Grunden,
is available through Amazon.com.*

www.ingramcontent.com/pod-product-compliance
Lightning Source LLC
Chambersburg PA
CBHW060501010526
44118CB00018B/2495